Celebrating Abundance

Other seasonal and daily reflections from
Walter Brueggemann

A Way Other than Our Own: Devotions for Lent

Names for the Messiah: An Advent Study

Gift and Task: A Year of Daily Readings and Reflections

Celebrating Abundance

Devotions for Advent

Walter Brueggemann

Compiled by Richard Floyd

WESTMINSTER
JOHN KNOX PRESS
LOUISVILLE · KENTUCKY

© 2017 Walter Brueggemann

First edition
Published by Westminster John Knox Press
Louisville, Kentucky

17 18 19 20 21 22 23 24 25 26—10 9 8 7 6 5 4 3 2 1

Unless otherwise indicated, Scripture quotations are from the New Revised Standard Version of the Bible, copyright © 1989 by the Division of Christian Education of the National Council of the Churches of Christ in the U.S.A., and are used by permission.

Some content has been previously published in Walter Brueggemann, *The Collected Sermons of Walter Brueggemann*, vols. 1 and 2 (Louisville, KY: Westminster John Knox Press, 2011, 2015) and is used by permission.

Book design by Sharon Adams
Cover design by Eric Walljasper

Library of Congress Cataloging-in-Publication Data

Names: Brueggemann, Walter, author. | Floyd, Richard A., author.
Title: Celebrating abundance : devotions for advent / Walter Brueggemann ; compiled by Richard Floyd.
Description: First edition. | Louisville, Kentucky : Westminster John Knox Press, [2017] |
Identifiers: LCCN 2017005506 (print) | LCCN 2017029149 (ebook) | ISBN 9781611648249 (ebk.) | ISBN 9780664262273 (pbk. : alk. paper)
Subjects: LCSH: Advent--Prayers and devotions.
Classification: LCC BV40 (ebook) | LCC BV40 .B757 2017 (print) | DDC 242/.332--dc23
LC record available at https://lccn.loc.gov/2017005506

Most Westminster John Knox Press books are available at special quantity discounts when purchased in bulk by corporations, organizations, and special-interest groups. For more information, please e-mail SpecialSales@wjkbooks.com.

Contents

Week Three

Week Four

Prayers for the Christmas Season

Compiler's Note

Advent is a time for telling the truth—the truth of our weariness and our anxiety, yes, but also the truth of the relentless generosity of God, which opens up futures that seem to be shut down. Walter Brueggemann is a persistent truth-teller, and his sermons invite us to consider the newness and abundance of God that is always already breaking into our settled lives.

If Advent is also a time for waking up, consider Walter an indefatigable alarm clock.

In the prayers that follow each entry, I have tried to draw on Walter's own language and imagery. May they be an occasion to enter more deeply into the text and the season of Advent.

Richard Floyd

Week One

Newness Is on Its Way

> As the people were filled with expectation, and all
> were questioning in their hearts concerning John,
> whether he might be the Messiah, John answered
> all of them by saying, "I baptize you with water;
> but one who is more powerful than I is coming; I
> am not worthy to untie the thong of his sandals.
> He will baptize you with the Holy Spirit and fire."
> —Luke 3:15–16

John the Baptizer bursts upon the Gospel of Luke. That is because it is Advent time. And whenever it is Advent time, we get John. It is not yet time for Jesus. This is still the time for getting ready. Getting ready time is not mainly about busy activity, entertaining, and fatigue. Getting ready time is mainly abrasive . . . asking, thinking, pondering, and redeciding.

"He will baptize you with the Holy Spirit and fire" (v. 16). Now I imagine that sounds as weird to you as it does to me. We who are relatively affluent and relatively sophisticated do not talk that way and do not welcome it. In truth, however, being baptized with God's holy spirit does not mean charismatic acting out. It means, I take it, we may be visited by a spirit of openness, generosity, energy, that "the force" may come over us, carry us to do obedient things we have not yet done, kingdom things we did not think we had in us, neighbor things from which we cringe. The whole tenor of Advent is that God may act in us, through us, beyond us, more than we imagined, because newness is on its way among us.

John is not the newness. He prepares us for the newness. And his word is that if we want to be immersed in the life-giving power of God, then we must *do* as John says: Share your coat and shoes and goods . . . Manage money in neighborly ways . . . Quit being the heavy in social transactions.

Who would have thought such concrete acts are the tactic whereby God's newness will yet come! Advent is not the kind of "preparation" that involves shopping and parties and cards. Such illusions of abundance disguise the true cravings of our weary souls. Advent is preparation for the demands of newness that will break the tired patterns of fear in our lives.

It is no wonder that in the very next verses of Luke 3, King Herod arrested John, imprisoned him, and tried to silence him. For what John says was dangerous for business as usual. Herod and his company preferred to imagine that their established credentials were enough, with Abraham as their father. And anyway, they did not want newness, so they tried to stop the dangerous newness before it ever intruded into their lives.

What we know, that Herod didn't know and never even suspected, is that John's Advent invitation cannot be silenced or arrested. It continues to invite. And sometimes we let it come among us and transform us.

> *Living God, visit us in this season with your Holy Spirit that we may get carried away to do obedient things we have not yet done, kingdom things we did not think we had in us, neighbor things from which we cringe. May you act in us, through us, beyond us, more than we imagine, because newness is on its way among us. Amen.*

Outrageous God

For I am about to create new heavens
    and a new earth;
the former things shall not be remembered
    or come to mind.
But be glad and rejoice forever
    in what I am creating;
for I am about to create Jerusalem as a joy,
    and its people as a delight.
I will rejoice in Jerusalem,
    and delight in my people;
no more shall the sound of weeping be heard
      in it,
    or the cry of distress.
            —Isaiah 65:17–19

I invite you to entertain for a moment this poem and let it seep into your bones, and into your heart, and into your vision. God speaks: "New heaven, new earth, new Jerusalem." It will be a world of rejoicing when the newness comes. And you know why?

Heaven and earth will rejoice because in that new world wrought by God, there will be no more the sound of weeping, no more homeless folks to moan, no more broken folk to whimper, no more terrorized folk to cry out.

Heaven and earth will rejoice, because in that new world wrought by God there will be no more infant mortality, no more infants who live but a few days, and no more old people who will die too young or live too feebly or continue as a shell while the life is gone.

Heaven and earth will rejoice, because in that new world wrought by God there will be no more usurpation of peoples' homes. Those who build will stay around to inhabit, those who plant will survive to harvest and enjoy their produce. No more people being taxed out of their homes, no more losing their vulnerable homes to the right of eminent domain, no more rapacious seizure by war. When the newness comes, every person will live safely under a vine and fig tree, safe, unafraid, at peace, with no more destructive threats or competitive anxieties.

Heaven and earth will rejoice, because in that new world wrought by God, God will be attentive. God will be like a mother who hears and answers in the night, knowing before we call who is needed and what is needed. And we shall never be left alone again.

The poem is outrageous. The new world of God is beyond our capacity and even beyond our imagination. It does not seem possible. In our fatigue, our self-sufficiency, and our cynicism, we deeply believe that such promises could not happen here. Such newness is only poetic fantasy.

In Advent, however, we receive the power of God that lies beyond us. This power is the antidote to our fatigue and cynicism. It is the gospel resolution to our spent self-sufficiency, when we are at the edge of our coping. It is the good news that will overmatch our cynicism that imagines there is no new thing that can enter our world.

> *Outrageous God, outflank our weary Christmas*
> *with the Advent miracle of a power that lies*
> *beyond us. May we receive this power, this new*
> *vision, which would set us free to live boldly into*
> *your dream for the world. Amen.*

Celebrating the New Abundance

> And all ate and were filled; and they took up
> twelve baskets full of broken pieces and of the fish.
> —Mark 6:42–43

In the Gospel of Mark, in chapter 6, Jesus does one of his most impressive miracles, that is, a transformative event to exhibit the saving power of God that is present in and through his life. It is the narrative of feeding the five thousand people. Mark tells us that Jesus had gone with his disciples apart to pray, but huge crowds followed him. Jesus saw the crowds and reacted in kindness to them. He saw their need, and he was moved by compassion for them. He wanted to make their life better. First he taught them the good news of God's generous love. And then he fed them . . . all five thousand of them.

The disciples didn't understand, of course, and thought he couldn't feed such a big crowd. So he took the five loaves and the two fish . . . that is one man's lunch. He took what was there, but then he acted on what was there in his lordly, compassionate, generous way. He turns ordinary food into a sacramental sign of God's massive goodness and generosity. Mark reports:

> Taking the five loaves and the two fish, he looked
> up to heaven, and blessed and broke the loaves, and
> gave them to his disciples to set before the people.
> (Mark 6:41)

The words sound familiar, do they not? His prayer consists in the four big verbs of Holy Communion: "He took, he blessed, he broke, he gave." Jesus takes the ordinary stuff of life in all its scarcity—two fish and five loaves—and transforms them into God's self-giving generosity. The outcome was that "all ate and were filled" (v. 42). But that is not all: there were twelve baskets left over, enough bread for all the tribes of Israel.

The church—the disciples—are always a little slow, unwilling to learn what the new data of Jesus means, unwilling to recognize that the world is changed by Jesus, unable to act differently in the new world of Jesus. The disciples seem often to act as though Jesus did not really matter; they act as though the world were still bound in scarcity and anxiety and fearfulness and hoarding.

But let me tell you the news that is proclaimed in Christ's coming, about which we are reminded at every Communion service: Jesus has turned the world into abundance. God is the gift who keeps on giving, and the people around Jesus are empowered to receive abundance and therefore to act generously.

Every day, all day: it's still true! "He takes, he blesses, he breaks, he gives." And we are astonished about the surplus. It is all there for those with eyes to see, with ears to hear, and with hearts to remember. We are recipients of enough and enough and more than enough, enough and enough and more than enough to share. And to be glad in this Giver who keeps on giving . . . endlessly.

> *God whose giving knows no end, make us glad*
> *recipients of your generosity. Give us eyes to see and*
> *ears to hear and hearts to remember your abundance,*
> *that we might share it with the world. Amen.*

The Vicious Cycle Broken

He shall judge between the nations,
and shall arbitrate for many peoples;
they shall beat their swords into plowshares,
and their spears into pruning hooks;
nation shall not lift up sword against nation,
neither shall they learn war any more.
—Isaiah 2:4

It is written in Deuteronomy that the poor will always be with you (Deut. 15:11). It is written elsewhere that there will always be wars and rumors of wars. It is written in the American psyche that the big ones will always eat the little ones. It is written in the hearts of many hurting ones that their situation will always be abusive and exploitative. It is written and it is believed and it is lived, that the world is a hostile, destructive place. You must be on guard and maintain whatever advantage you can. It is written and recited like a mantra, world without end.

In the middle of that hopelessness, Advent issues a vision of another day, written by the poet, given to Israel midst the deathly cadence. We do not know when, but we know for sure. The poet knows for sure that this dying and killing is not forever, because another word has been spoken. Another decision has been made. A word has been given that shatters our conventions, which bursts open the prospect for life in a world of death. The poem lingers with dangerous power, even for us, even now.

Watch that vision, because it ends in a dramatic moment of transformation. The old city is full of black-smiths who have so much work to do. Listen and you can hear the hammer on the anvil. The smiths are beating and pounding iron, reshaping it, beating swords into plowshares and spears into tools for orchards. They are decontaminating bombs and defusing the great weapons systems. The fear is dissipating. The hate is collapsing. The anxiety is lessening. The buildup of competitive threat is being reversed. The nations are returning to their proper vocation—care of the earth, love of creation, bounty for neighbor, enough for all, with newness, deep joy, hard work, all because the vicious cycles are ended and life becomes possible.

This vision sounds impossible. It sounded impossible the first time it was uttered; it has not become more realistic in the meantime. Advent, nonetheless, is a time for a new reality. It is not the poem but the old power arrangements of deathliness that are unrealistic. They are unrealistic among the nations and in our communities and churches and families. There is a new possibility now among us, rooted in God's love and God's suffering power. Power from God's love breaks the vicious cycles. We have seen them broken in Jesus, and occasionally we have seen them broken in our own lives. It is promised that the cycles can be broken, disarmament will happen, and life can be different. It is promised and it is coming, in God's good time.

God of love and suffering power, speak again your
word of transformation in the midst of our weary
world. We so easily capitulate to despair, to numb
acceptance of deathly orders. Break the vicious
cycles, and kindle in us once again a passion for the
possible. Amen.

Season of Decrease

The wolf and the lamb shall feed together,
　　the lion shall eat straw like the ox;
　　　but the serpent—its food shall be dust!
They shall not hurt or destroy
　　on all my holy mountain,
　　　says the LORD.

—Isaiah 65:25

"He must increase, but I must decrease."
—John the Baptist, in John 3:30

Into this season pushes the unkempt, unwelcome figure of John the Baptizer. You remember him. He is dressed in a hair shirt. He eats wild honey and such other gifts that he can forage in the rough.

He comes in anger and demanding, with threats and insistence. He speaks really only one word: *Repent!* Recognize the danger you are in and change. In the Gospel narrative, John embodies the best and the last of the old tradition of Torah demand. He has this deep sense of urgency about the world, but it is not an urgency of newness. It is an urgency of threat and danger and jeopardy, one that we ourselves sense now about our world. He comes first in the story. He comes before Jesus. He is the key player in the Advent narrative.

When Jesus appears on the scene, John the Baptizer immediately acknowledges the greatness of Jesus, greater than all that is past—greater than John, greater than all ancient memories and hopes. When Jesus comes into the narrative, John quickly, abruptly, without reservation says of Jesus, "He must increase, but I must decrease."

What to do while we watch and wait this Advent season? Move from the large vision of Isaiah to the small discipline of John. If John embodies all that is old and Jesus embodies all that is new, take as your Advent work toward Christmas that enterprise: decrease/increase. Decrease what is old and habitual and destructive in your life so that the new life-giving power of Jesus may grow large with you: Decrease what is greedy, what is frantic consumerism, for the increase of simple, life-giving sharing. Decrease what is fearful and defensive, for the increase of life-giving compassion and generosity. Decrease what is fraudulent and pretense, for the increase of life-giving truth-telling in your life, truth-telling about you and your neighbor, about the sickness of our society and our enmeshment in that sickness. Decrease what is hateful and alienating, for the increase of healing and forgiveness, which finally are the only source of life.

Advent basks in the great promises. In the meantime, however, there are daily disciplines, day-to-day exercises of Advent, work that requires time and intentionality. Advent is not a time of casual waiting. It is a demanding piece of work. It requires both the outrageousness of God and the daily work of decreasing so that Jesus and God's vision of peace may increase.

> *In this season of Advent, open our hearts to receive the hard word of repentance. Empower us to decrease what is old, habitual, and destructive in our lives so that the new life-giving power of Jesus may grow large within us. Amen.*

The Poem: Subversion and Summons

They will not hurt or destroy
on all my holy mountain;
for the earth will be full of the knowledge of the
LORD
as the waters cover the sea.

—Isaiah 11:9

In poetry we can do things not permitted by logic or reason. Poetry will open the world beyond reason. Poetry will give access to contradictions and tensions that logic must deny. Poetry will not only remember but also propose and conjure and wonder and imagine and foretell.

So Jews, in their covenantal fidelity, did poems. Miriam did poetry when they crossed out of Egyptian slavery. Deborah did poetry when it dawned on them that the Canaanites were not so formidable. Hannah did poetry when little Samuel was born. Eventually Mary did poetry when she found out she was pregnant. All these mothers in Israel celebrated the impossible that was right before their eyes, even though they could explain none of it. They did poetry while the hard men were still parsing logic, writing memos to each other, and drafting briefs.

I propose that Advent is a time of struggle between the poem that opens the future that God will work and the memo that keeps control. Advent is a time for relinquishing some of the control in order to receive the impossible from God.

> The wolf shall live with the lamb,
>   the leopard shall lie down with the kid,
> the calf and the lion and the fatling together,
>   and a little child shall lead them.
> The cow and the bear shall graze,
>   their young shall lie down together;
>   and the lion shall eat straw like the ox.
>
> (vv. 6–7)

The old enmities, the old appetites of the food chain, the old assumptions of the survival of the meanest, all of that is subverted. The wild will not stay vicious, because the coming one, marked by righteousness and justice, will overrule raw power in the interest of new possibility. Finally, the young child will toy with the asp and the adder; nobody will get hurt, because the poison will be removed from the world. The poison will be gone because the shoot will override all business as usual. All will be well, and all manner of thing will be well.

The poem is about advent, about the coming one. And we dare to say, we confessing Christians, that the poem concerns the Christmas baby who refuses Rome's rule of force and religion's rule of code, opening the world to healing, freedom, forgiveness, and joy. So try this in Advent: depart from logic and memo and syllogism, and host the poem.

> *Break open our imaginations this Advent, O God,*
> *so that we might see a world decisively shaped by*
> *your fidelity. Aid us in relinquishing control in*
> *order to receive your newness. Amen.*

Glory in the Wilderness

They shall see the glory of the LORD,
　　the majesty of our God.
　　　　　　　　　　　　　—Isaiah 35:2

"The voice of one crying out in the wilderness:
'Prepare the way of the Lord,
　　make his paths straight.'"
　　　　　　　　　　　　　—Matthew 3:3b

Advent is the season when we await the coming of God's glory, which has not yet come. Glory. Since the word is so odd, we may wonder exactly what it is that we wait for. We may even ask if we would know it if we saw it.

The glory of Yahweh is not simply bland, ordinary, enthusiastic religion. Affirmation of God's glory is always a counter-statement. It is not only pro-Yahweh, but it is also determinedly *anti*. We do not know what to sing for if we do not understand what we sing against. The glory of God is not sung in a vacuum but in a context where much is at risk.

The context, according to this poem, is the wilderness and the desert. The wilderness is a place where the power for life is fragile and diminished. The inhabitants of the desert are those with weak hands and feeble knees and fearful hearts, those who have had their vitality crushed and their authority nullified and their will for life nearly defeated. This poem is a roll call of the marginalized, the blind, the deaf, the lame, the dumb, all the disabled. The wilderness is a place where the power for life is fragile and diminished.

It is Advent time in the wilderness. Shriveled up earth and crushed down humanity wait for the coming, in the wilderness. It is no wonder that John quotes Isaiah, "Prepare in the wilderness a special way." It is no wonder that John, in anticipation of Jesus, says, "They shall all see the glory." They shall all see God's massiveness and power that transforms. The wonder and the oddness is that in the shadow of that great glory comes the protected, rescued, vulnerable, valued ones who travel for the first time in safety and in joy. There finally is *shalom* on earth, even in the desert. The choirs, however, never sing of *shalom* on earth, until they first celebrate the *glory*. The *shalom* of the desert follows from the glory of God.

In Advent, we know about the God who transforms, makes new, and begins again. No wonder creation and humanity, one at a time, all together, sing of the new world bursting with the abundant glory of God.

> *Too often we have become inured to the wilderness,*
> *O God, to the fragility and diminishment of life.*
> *But Advent is the season of your coming. May*
> *we celebrate your glory and sing of your* shalom.
> *Amen.*

Week Two

Energy at Midpoint

But those who wait for the LORD shall renew
    their strength,
      they shell mount up with wings like eagles,
    they shall run and not be weary,
      they shall walk and not faint.
                    —Isaiah 40:31

The poem in Isaiah 40 is a poem addressed to the Israelites in Babylonian exile. They were displaced persons who had to believe in an alien environment, and that is not unlike our situation. The American Church increasingly is in an alien, hostile environment if it takes the claims of the gospel with real seriousness. The folks in Isaiah 40 were unclear about how to be God's people in such a situation, for it was more costly and dangerous than they wanted to face.

The poem reflects a faith community in which the possibilities of the gospel seem to have failed. We might call it burnout. They could not generate the old vitality. Nothing seemed to work. In this world, appeal to the power of God didn't carry much weight.

And then the poet makes a move to his listeners. The poet speaks about the people who trust in this God and who notice what God is doing. It is not only that God does not grow faint. It is that God gives power to the faint, and to he who has no might, God increases strength. The news in this poem is for the faint in the church, those who have run out of steam, out of patience, out of courage, out of imagination, out of generosity.

The reason we have run out is that we have believed the world too much. We have listened to the Babylonians. We have yearned too much for the American dream. And people who get caught in Babylonian dreams or American dreams wind up without energy for faith and mission.

But as we focus on the God who is free and restless and at work, we break the spell of the empire, and we are free again.

I saw a sign recently which said that God wants spiritual eagles, not chickens. But whether we fly, run, or walk, we are free, joyous, buoyant, ready to defy the empire, ready to receive God's gifts, ready to do God's will. Advent is a time for remembering and gratitude. But it is also for hoping, for receiving energy, for resolve for the mission. The mission is very tough these days. But God is not hidden, not indifferent, not powerless, and we are the people of this God.

So, dear eagles—soar into your mission. It is time to move toward the things we know best. They are our very life, and to them we are summoned: justice, mercy, compassion, peace. All you who are weary and are heavily laden, take the yoke of Christ—rest and obey!

> *By your loving spirit, may Advent be a time*
> *of remembering and giving thanks, and also a*
> *time of renewing our energy and our resolve for*
> *mission. May we rest and obey. Amen.*

The New Song

Sing to the LORD a new song,
    his praise from the end of the earth!
Let the sea roar and all that fills it,
    the coastlands and their inhabitants.
Let the desert and its towns lift up their voice,
    the villages that Kedar inhabits;
let the inhabitants of Sela sing for joy,
    let them shout from the tops of the
        mountains.
                    —Isaiah 42:10–11

Can you imagine writing this poem and singing this song in exile? Can you imagine defying the empire by sketching out this daring alternative? Can you dare to sing this song under the very nose of Babylonian soldiers, about a new reality that counters the empire? Think of it, new reality conjured in worship, by the choir, inviting to new courage, new faith, new energy, new obedience, new joy.

You see, the song is as subversive as is the new reality. The new song never describes the world the way it now is. The new song imagines how the world will be in God's good time to come. The new song is a protest against the way the world now is. The new song is a refusal to accept the present world as it is, a refusal to believe this is right or that the present will last. The church is always at its most daring and risking and dangerous and free when it sings a new song. Because then it sings that the power of the gospel will not let the world finally stay as it is.

We are not unlike those ancient exiles, scattered where we do not have much impact, sensing that the world is resistant to change, aware that the policies and practices all around us are aimed at death. We are close to despair in our weakness and futility.

About many things, it appears that not much can be done. When this community of faith could do very little, however, it did not resign itself to playing it safe. Instead, it sang new songs, counter songs that refused to let the promise of the gospel sink into the landscape of the empire. The new song is a protest. The new song is also a bold assertion, innocently declaring that the God of the gospel has plans and purposes and a will to reorder the world, to bring wholeness and health to the blind, the poor, the needy, to the nations so fearful, and to the entire creation now so under killing assault. The song asserts God's future against our present tense.

It is no wonder, once the singing begins, that all creation sings and dances and claps with us. The whole of creation sings a new song about God's new world. Heaven and nature sing and earth repeats the loud amen. We sing the song, even in exile, then we live the new reality. The Babylonians cannot stop us, because the song is true and more powerful than the tearfulness of the world. The exiles are indeed on their way—rejoicing.

> *In this Advent season, teach us the new song,*
> *which heralds the new world that is coming, the*
> *new reality that is taking shape before our eyes.*
> *May we rejoice in its truth and power and join all*
> *creation in its loud amen! Amen!*

Transformative Solidarity

Be mindful of your mercy, O LORD, and of your
    steadfast love,
  for they have been from of old.
Do not remember the sins of my youth or my
    transgressions;
  according to your steadfast love remember me,
  for your goodness sake, O LORD!

Good and upright is the LORD;
  therefore he instructs sinners in the way.
He leads the humble in what is right,
  and teaches the humble his way.
All the paths of the LORD are steadfast love and
    faithfulness,
  for those who keep his covenant and his
    decrees.
                    —Psalm 25:6–10

The Psalmist revels in God's mercy, goodness, and steadfast love. It is the same term three times, *steadfast love*, a term always on the lips of ancient Israel, a term that most fully characterizes the God of Christmas for whom we prepare in Advent. *Steadfast love* means solidarity in need enacted with transformative strength. It is the solidarity enacted with strength that Israel knows in the exodus and in a thousand other life-giving miracles.

It is the solidarity in need offered by Jesus to the woman at the well, to the tax man in the tree, to the blind beggar, to the woman with a bad back. What human persons and human community most need is abiding, committed, passionate *transformative solidarity*. This psalmist waits for it in need and knows the place from where it comes.

Truth to tell, that kind of solidarity is not on offer in our world from the big players in power and money and authority. Israel knew that it was not on offer from Pharaoh, who always demanded productivity. Jesus knew it was not on offer from Pilate, who washed his hands of need. It is not on offer by most of the loud voices of ideology and propaganda among us.

Imagine a whole company of believers rethinking their lives, redeploying their energy, reassessing their purposes. The path is *to love God*, not party, not ideology, not pet project, but God's will for steadfast love that is not deterred by fear and anxiety. The path is *to love neighbor*, to love neighbor face-to-face, to love neighbor in community action, to love neighbor in systemic arrangements, in imaginative policies.

The decrees of Caesar Augustus continue to go out for taxes and for draft and for frantic attempts to keep the world under our control. But the truth is found in the vulnerable village of Bethlehem outside the capital city, the village that disregarded the imperial decree. It will take a village to exhibit this alternative, and we are citizens of that coming society.

> *In the midst of a tired and fearful word, we have heard the promise of your steadfast love, your transformative solidarity. May we wait with eager longing for the one thing needed, for the one source that assures. May we be in readiness for your coming, O God. Amen.*

A Secret World of Possibility

At that same hour Jesus rejoiced in the Holy Spirit and said, "I thank you, Father, Lord of heaven and earth, because you have hidden these things from the wise and the intelligent and have revealed them to infants; yes, Father, for such was your gracious will." . . . Then turning to the disciples, Jesus said to them privately, "Blessed are the eyes that see what you see! For I tell you that many prophets and kings desired to see what you see, but did not see it, and to hear what you hear, but did not hear it."

—Luke 10:21, 23–24

Jesus was always the teacher, always wanting his disciples to understand better what he was up to. The problem was that much of what he told them did not fit their categories, so they were more often bewildered by his teaching rather than illuminated. It turned out, as they came to understand only later, that he was talking about another world than the one they thought they had in hand. It is something of a secret world, deliberately hidden from those who think they already know everything and control everything.

Jesus blurts out this remarkably enigmatic statement, "Blessed are the eyes that see what you see" (v. 23). After he said this, he extended his claim about odd seeing even further: "For I tell you that many prophets and kings desired to see what you see, but did not see it, and to hear what you hear, but did not hear it" (v. 24).

The disciples are contrasted with the best minds culture can provide, with prophets and with kings. Prophets are those who are thought to have entry into supernatural mysteries, and kings are those who have all the power, central surveillance, and intelligence, and therefore access to everything. Naive like babies, the disciples have access, so says Jesus, that neither prophets nor kings, neither the humanists nor the scientists, have penetrated.

Throughout the Bible, there is an argument about the nature of social reality. On the face of it, it was evident that the wise knew best, and the powerful were in control, and the shrewd would always win. There is lots of evidence for such a view. But the Bible keeps stirring the pot, raising questions, and giving hints that in the mercy and power of God, this is not quite an accurate reading of the world. There is a kind of power exercised by the weak, that is liberating and transformative. If you do not want to miss out, you must pay attention to that other world, that unreasonable, inexplicable world saturated with God's holiness, that is in the long run more decisive and more satisfying than the available world offers.

> *O Lord, open us more and more to this alternative world in which your grace and power are revealed through the weak and the vulnerable. May we find our deep satisfaction in that unreasonable, inexplicable world saturated by your holiness. Amen.*

An Alternative World at Hand

> For whatever was written in former days was written for our instruction, so that by steadfastness and by the encouragement of the scriptures we might have hope. May the God of steadfastness and encouragement grant you to live in harmony with one another, in accordance with Christ Jesus, so that together you may with one voice glorify the God and Father of our Lord Jesus Christ.
>
> —Romans 15:4–6

Here is the good news I am privileged to announce to you. There is a new world available that is here very soon. It is being birthed in the wonder of Jesus of Nazareth. It is a world marked by the stable smell of shepherds and the perfumes of the wise men. It is a world marked by a Friday of suffering and death and by a Sunday of surprise and new life. It is a world that exposes all the contradictions of our present life. It is a world that invites us to move out from here to there in joy, in obedience, in discipline, to begin again.

As Paul spoke of the truthful reliability of God's promise, he knew about a world of fickle deception and betrayal, as do we. The world of advertising, of ideology, of euphemism offers us endless phoniness that coerces and manipulates and invites into a virtual world that has no staying power. You cannot count on such a world, as it will turn on you and cost you dearly. And yet, out beyond that fickle world there is the world of God's reliable fidelity, a God who makes and keeps promises, and you can dwell there.

As Paul envisioned welcome of one another, he knew about a world of exclusion that is grounded in fear and anxiety. And so do we. All around now are barriers and gates and fences that draw lines around gifts and possibilities and resources and access. The lines are drawn closer and closer until all are excluded except the blessed, cunning ones, and even they are left nervous about when the next wall will be built and who will then be excluded. And yet, out beyond the world of exclusion and rejection and hostility, there is on offer a world of welcome that sees the other not as threat or competitor but as cohort on the pilgrimage of humanity.

When Paul spoke about living in harmony with one another as a gift of Christ's new regime, he knew about conflict and quarreling in his churches and all around the empire. And so do we. We imagine now that liberals and conservatives must be in conflict, and Christians and Muslims must be in shared violence with each other, and poor blacks and rich whites must compete with an edge of hate. And yet, out beyond there is a world reconciled between Jew and Greek, between male and female, between free and slave, and all the other alienations that we can name. Because Christ has broken down the walls of separation. In him all sorts of people recover their sanity and their humanity enough to see brother and sister.

> *Grant us, reconciling God, the imagination with*
> *which to see the world coming into being through*
> *the wonder of Jesus of Nazareth. May we embrace*
> *it and dwell there in joy, in obedience, in discipline,*
> *to begin again. Amen.*

Baffled by Abundance

> But when they saw him walking on the sea, they
> thought it was a ghost and cried out; for they all
> saw him and were terrified. But immediately he
> spoke to them and said, "Take heart, it is I; do
> not be afraid." Then he got into the boat with
> them and the wind ceased. And they were utterly
> astounded, for they did not understand about the
> loaves, but their hearts were hardened.
>
> Mark 6:49–52

Earlier in this text, Jesus has just performed his great
drama of abundance. He took the loaves and the fish.
He blessed them, he broke them, and he gave them. He
did his four big defining verbs: "he took, he blessed, he
broke, he gave." There was enough bread for five thousand men and twelve baskets of surplus. Loaves abound!

But then, as Mark likes to say, "immediately," they
were in a boat with an adverse wind; they were strain-
ing at the oars against the wind. He came toward them—
this agent of abundance—in the middle of the storm.
He walked atop the waters, right on the surface of surly
chaos. He is the ruler of the chaos that jeopardized them.
He surprised them and scared them, because he was not
where they expected him to be. They never expected him
to glide over chaos. They did not expect to see him amid
the storm. They surely did not expect to see him amid
chaos that had, until he showed, seemed so threatening.

"Immediately," he spoke to them. He said, "Have courage!" It is I; do not fear. He spoke the classic assurance of calm, the one Isaiah spoke to the exiles, the one the angels spoke to the shepherds at the birth, the one the angel will speak at the empty Easter tomb, the one every parent speaks in the midst of a child's nightmare: "Do not be afraid. I am right here." Do not fear; it is I. I am in the midst of the storm; I who tamed hunger can manage chaos.

Mark adds a verse to explain why the disciples were terrified, why they lacked confidence in him, and why they lacked categories through which to discern his transformative power. They could not understand about the loaves, twelve baskets surplus wrought out of five loaves and a few fish. They could not understand that the lord of abundance had changed everything. And they could not understand because their hearts were hard or dull or obtuse or blind. They were not about to engage in the new reality in front of them.

Well, here is the news. God's spirit is at work on heart transplants! God's spirit is at work on you and me and all of us, in many ways, relieving us of old hearts that have become too hard to function properly. The God who can produce surplus bread and still storms is the God who can make new our primal organ of humanness. Who would have thought that out of stony hearts there might come peace?

> *We confess that we are inured to chaos, O God.*
> *We are well accustomed to fear and scarcity, and*
> *so we do not easily discern your transformative*
> *power. Make our hardened hearts supple once*
> *again, so that we might be prepared to celebrate*
> *the lord of abundance. Amen.*

Hopeful Along with the Others

> For a child has been born for us,
>   a son given to us;
> authority rests upon his shoulders;
>   and he is named
> Wonderful Counselor, Mighty God,
>   Everlasting Father, Prince of Peace.
> His authority shall grow continually,
>   and there shall be endless peace
> for the throne of David and his kingdom.
>   He will establish and uphold it
> with justice and with righteousness
>   from this time onward and forevermore.
> The zeal of the LORD of hosts will do this.
>
> —Isaiah 9:6–7

What Jews and Christians have in common—alone and with no one else—is that we believe that there is one who is coming to make the world right. We believe that God has not given up on God's own will for the world and God's promise to make the world whole and safe and peaceable. We believe that this one who is to come to make all things new and good and safe and whole is *a human agent*, a human person who is committed to God's way. We believe that the dreams of heaven will come to be earthly reality, which is why we pray regularly, "Your kingdom come, your will be done on earth as it is in heaven."

What distinguishes Christians from all others—including Jews—is that we believe that this one who is to come from God has already come and begun his work. It is *Jesus of Nazareth*. We call him Christ, which is a Greek translation of the Jewish word "messiah."

Since the very earliest church, we Christians have watched Jesus, and we have seen his work: We have listened to his teaching and noticed his wisdom. We have noticed his attentiveness to the needs of the poor and the lame and the blind and the lepers. We have watched as he gives new life where none seemed possible. We have noticed and concluded that God's power for life is present in Jesus, and we believe—as Jews wait for Messiah—that this Messiah-Christ, Jesus, will come again to make the world right.

Do I need to tell you that waiting for this man from God is what Christmas is all about? Do I need to tell you that Christmas is a time to ponder and notice what has already begun of this new age, because Jesus has already been here? Do I need to remind you that in baptism, we Christians have signed on for the work of justice and righteousness and compassion and forgiveness that is the hallmark of God's presence in Jesus? That waiting and doing gives us a plate full of joy and work, without being overburdened with the excessive Christmas demands of our culture? We believe that. We believe God is keeping his promises even among us in our time and place.

> *In this season, we look to the hope of the Scripture and trust that you are not through with this world. As we await Jesus's coming anew, fill us with your Spirit to do the work of justice, righteousness, compassion, and forgiveness in our time and place. Amen.*

Week Three

The *What* and the *When* of the Christ Child

To you, O LORD, I lift up my soul.
O my God, in you I trust;
　　do not let me be put to shame;
　　do not let my enemies exult over me.
Do not let those who wait for you be put to
　　　　shame;
　　let them be ashamed who are wantonly
　　　　treacherous.

Make me to know your ways, O LORD;
　　teach me your paths.
Lead me in your truth, and teach me,
　　for you are the God of my salvation;
　　for you I wait all day long.
　　　　　　　　　　　　—Psalm 25:1–5

People like us have careful work to do in Advent, to weave our way between two big dangers. On the one hand, there are dangerous people floating around the church who specialize in times and dates and schedules, who know with precision the time of Christ's coming and who speak confidently of millennia and pre-millennia and post-millennia. They know too much and reduce God's freedom to the timetable of their ideology.

On the other hand, there are dangerous people floating around the church who are offended by those people and who in reaction are in love with their comfortable affluence, imagine that it will not get any better than this, and expect no gospel arrival at any time ever. People like us live in that awkward place amid those *who know too much* and those *who expect nothing*. We occupy a different posture about Advent as we ready for Christmas. We are the ones who know *what* is coming but do not know *when*.

The *what* for which we wait at Christmas and for which we prepare in Advent is that God's rule of starchy justice and generous mercy will arise in the earth, and all that seek to negate abundant life will be overruled and nullified. That is how we pray every time we are together. We pray, "Thy kingdom come, thy will be done." We pray that God would show God's self so that the power of chaos and death, of greed and brutality, of selfishness and hate would end, for such negators cannot stay when God comes among us. We pray always in confidence, for we end and say, "For yours is the kingdom and the power and the glory" . . . it belongs to no one else.

But we do not know the *when*. We do not know when because the coming of God is not our doing. God's way is a mystery that has not been entrusted to us. It is hard for us to imagine that the regime of violent death will finally not prevail, and we do not know when or how it will end, because we trust all of that to God.

> *At times we know too much, shrinking your possibility to fit our narrow imaginings. At times we expect nothing new, wrapping ourselves in despair to fend off your newness. But this Advent season, may we think deeply and face passionately the "what" of your way, O God, without any anxiety about the "when." Amen.*

A Catalog of Newnesses

> When John heard in prison what the Messiah was doing, he sent word by his disciples and said to him, "Are you the one who is to come, or are we to wait for another?" Jesus answered them, "Go and tell John what you hear and see: the blind receive their sight, the lame walk, the lepers are cleansed, the deaf hear, the dead are raised, and the poor have good news brought to them. And blessed is anyone who takes no offense at me."
>
> —Matthew 11:2–6

The distance between John the Baptizer and Jesus is small, not more than a millimeter, but it is a space upon which our faith turns. It is the huge leap between *advent and preparation* and the *birth of newness* in the Christ. It is not more than an instant. It is quick and the world does not even notice. But it is the great leap of our life, moving from the *severity of the John season* to the *Jesus season*, and the leap makes a big difference.

The Jesus season for which we wait at Christmas, that we Christians count on and are baptized into, is a season of wondrous healing, of unexplained newness, of free gifts that will let us live whole, joyous lives. Jesus is too good to be true, and John his cousin cannot believe. John is something of a "theological terrorist" whom King Herod has imprisoned and charged with disturbing the peace. From his jail cell he sends an inquiry to this unbelievable cousin

Jesus: Are you the one who will make it all new? Are you for real? Should we count on Christmas?

Jesus answers, always prudent and cautious. I am not sure I am the one, because the creeds will not be written for a long while yet. But let me give you the data you need to make up your own mind about your question:

> "Go and tell John what you hear and see: the blind receive their sight, the lame walk, the lepers are cleansed, the deaf hear, the dead are raised, and the poor have good news brought to them." (Matt. 11:4–5)

Jesus offers a catalog of newnesses, of miracles, of wonders, transformations that take people in their fear and failure and disability, and wrap their lives in newness beyond themselves. That is what Jesus does. Everywhere he goes, newness happens. Newness and healing and well-being emit from his body wherever he is. That is what it means to live in the new world birthed at Christmas. John can draw his own conclusions, but this Jesus is surely doing everything promised, everything hoped for. Not bragging, just reporting on the birth of newness that the world cannot manufacture.

> *Prepare our hearts, O God, for the newness that is coming to the world. Open our eyes to the places it is breaking out in our world and in our lives, that we may know that we can count on Christmas. Amen.*

The *Yet* on the Other Side

As they went away, Jesus began to speak to the crowds about John: "What did you go out into the wilderness to look at? A reed shaken by the wind? What then did you go out to see? Someone dressed in soft robes? Look, those who wear soft robes are in royal palaces. What then did you go out to see? A prophet? Yes, I tell you, and more than a prophet. This is the one about whom it is written,

> 'See, I am sending my messenger ahead of you,
> who will prepare your way before you.'

Truly I tell you, among those born of women no one has arisen greater than John the Baptist; yet the least in the kingdom of heaven is greater than he."

—Matthew 11:7–11

J ohn is the one who gets everything ready; you cannot jump into the goodness of Christmas without readiness from him.

Did you think when you heard John that he would be a cowardly little guy? Jesus asks. That's not Advent. Did you expect when you saw him he would be all dressed up in fancy party clothes? Maybe for Christmas, but that's not Advent.

If you knew what he looked like, you would have expected a prophet. You know about prophets. They are Israel's *hopers*. They have their eye on God's future, the newness God will give. The prophets are Israel's *demanders* who keep reminding that you must face the demands of God's Torah commandments of justice and mercy and neighborliness, individual risks for the sake of the community. The prophets are Israel's greatest *summoners* who call Israel to change, to repent, to recruit away from the world's fast track, to the patient reality of neighborliness and humanness and compassion and justice . . .

Jesus knows his jailed cousin is crucial for getting ready. But after he speaks of John for a while, he reverses field. As if he said the hoper, the demander, the summoner is crucial, and you must pay attention. But I do not want you to pay so much attention to John and Advent that you do not notice the change in your life when the newness comes. John is a big public figure. Everyone knows about him, from King Herod on down. *Yet* the least in the kingdom is greater than John. What a footnote! No matter how crucial is the old moral urgency, the old disciplines of obedience and devotion, that produce good deeds and mercy and compassion, what comes at Bethlehem is greater. Greater are those who believe and practice the newness.

These weeks of Advent are a time to stand with John in jail and look to the newness. Imagine what it would be like to be least in newness and thereby greater than all the old arrangements.

This *yet* is our news. Jesus says, Let anyone who has ears, *listen*!

> *The newness of God is at hand! May we believe the newness, receive it, and practice it that we may share in the works of Jesus and live into the miracle that is surging around us. Amen.*

A New Governance Blown against Our Loss

A shoot shall come out from the stump of Jesse,
  and a branch shall grow out of his roots.
The spirit of the LORD shall rest on him,
    the spirit of wisdom and understanding,
    the spirit of counsel and might,
    the spirit of knowledge and the fear of the
    LORD.
—Isaiah 11:1–2

O ut of the stump that seemed dead, God will work a newness (v. 1). God will work a newness out of the wind—call it "spirit"—blowing life, bringing fresh possibility beyond our imagining: "The spirit of the LORD shall rest" (v. 2). The world began when the wind blew the waters back and let dry land appear. The world began when the wind of God blew (Gen. 1:2). It is such a wind that will baptize Jesus with power and authority, after all the old pedigrees of Abraham had failed and could produce no heirs and no future (Matt. 3:11). It is the same wind that blows against despair and unfaith and creates a church with power and courage (Acts 2:2–4). Such a wind creates worlds, empowers Jesus, makes the church possible. Such a wind—which we cannot explain or control or summon or resist—such a wind is the subject of this poem.

We know about endings of church, families, businesses, dynasties, even worlds. We know that our best arrangements grow feeble, gasp, and terminate. The endings are clear even when they hurt so much. Now in this poem, we know about beginnings from the only self-starter. The beginnings are so odd. Our faith counters the hurtful endings with this stupendous poem. Advent is a poem that imagines. You may think the poem is too flimsy and settle instead for realism, a realism that desperately tries to keep the ending propped up, so that we can fake it a little longer.

We baptized people, however, are not that in love with our loss. Instead we bet on the poet and on the poem, on the vision and on the possibility. No, we bet on the creative, generative, healing, transformative wind of God. Beyond loss—newness, beyond death—life. Beyond chaos—new creation, beyond, beyond, beyond, a wind, a spirit, a poem, new life. The blowing of newness is not ours. Ours is response, receptivity, repentance, good fruit, beginning again. We scarcely have language for the gift. But we notice the gift and the wind, and we move toward them with yearning. We go then with the child, the lions, the snakes, the lambs, the creatures, all creatures, created again, only by the wind. We come to know the child of David through whom that wind continues to blow new life!

> *God of the wind, open us once again to your power*
> *of newness. We know all about endings; we know*
> *all about the weariness that comes from propping*
> *up old realities. Free us for a new beginning this*
> *Advent season. Amen.*

A Dangerous Summons

From that time, Jesus began to proclaim, "Repent, for the kingdom of heaven has come near."

As he walked by the Sea of Galilee, he saw two brothers, Simon, who is called Peter, and Andrew his brother, casting a net into the sea— for they were fishermen. And he said to them, "Follow me, and I will make you fish for people." Immediately they left their nets and followed him.

—Matthew 4:17–20

The picture we are given in this text concerns the one who is a danger to the status quo and a threat to establishment powers; he comes in an intensely powerful way. When he gets there, he says three things that are characteristic slogans of the gospel movement:

1. *The Kingdom of Heaven is near.* Jesus is a revolutionary because he announces a takeover, a new regime. Some of his first hearers no doubt understood that he would displace Roman governance, which was an occupying force in Palestine that they hated. And so, they welcomed him. Since then, some have heard his coming and his announcement of a new regime as an overthrow of oppressive political powers, oppressions such as slavery and poverty and state violence, for Jesus challenges all such power arrangements. Since then some have heard his statement in more personal ways,

a new regime to combat addictions and guilts, old resentments that drain us and old hurts that nag at us and keep us from well-being. And now some may hear this as an invitation to break the endless rounds of greed and acquisitiveness, all that consumerism that destroys our society. Every old power of darkness and destructiveness is now on notice, because God's light is in the world in Jesus.

2. *Repent*. Just one word, a word too much tied up with our little moralisms. But in fact it is a very large word. It is an imperative word, change: change directions, change loyalty, change from guilt to compassion, change from self to neighbor, change from despair to buoyancy, change to the new governance. And they found that his very saying it empowered them to do it. The term is an imperative, but it is also an authorization. We are now authorized to quit serving the old governance, old systems, old fears, old guilts, old debts, freed by the coming of the light into the land of contempt and distress.

3. *Follow Me*. Jesus is looking for associates and assistants and comrades in the new governance that will displace the old. But to sign up and join in requires breaking loyalty to old patterns and old regimes. He did not nag or coerce. He expected that there was real readiness to leave what was for what is now coming to be. The light itself draws people out of their different darknesses, like insects drawn to the light.

Jesus the light is God's gift of new power for being human. Those fishermen by the Sea of Galilee went immediately into his new world. So might we!

> *God of a new day, you come to us in this season*
> *with the message of the kingdom and summon us*
> *to repent and follow. Draw us out of hopelessness*
> *into the gift of new power for a new life. Amen.*

Under New Management

> For I am about to create new heavens
>   and a new earth;
> the former things shall not be remembered
>   or come to mind.
>
> —Isaiah 65:17

L et me speak about the new heaven. That may seem strange and removed to you. And if it does not seem strange and irrelevant here, it does seem so almost everywhere else, for almost everyone, believer and unbeliever alike. For almost everyone assumes that heaven is either closed or empty and irrelevant. That is, almost everyone assumes the God question is closed or empty. Conservatives tend to think the God question is long ago settled and need not be reconsidered. And so we read the catechism. Liberals tend to think the God question is irrelevant and so leave that to someone else while we care for "the less fortunate." But isn't it strange that this poet uses his precious poetic gifts to speak of a new heaven? And he does so in a time of despair and stress in his community, when you would have thought he had other things to do. But he takes that as his proper task.

The newness that must be acknowledged is the bold recognition that we have to do with a new God, unlike any of the conventional gods who run the empire or who at least accommodate the empire. You know who most people think is in charge in heaven. Most people think that God in heaven is a self-serving consumer capitalist who, in his self-sufficiency, is entitled to have and take and devour, as long as he wants, with an insatiable appetite. And we order ourselves and run our economy on earth in the image of that God. The problem of earthly poverty will not be effectively overcome until the idol that justifies and legitimates greed as a cosmic reality is crushed to death. The news of the Bible is that a new power governs from on high, and the policies of that God are at edge of fulfillment on earth.

I dare to say to you that this poem is about as relevant as we can get, for it affirms to us that the current contrivance that makes some rich at the expense of others is a momentary contrivance. That contrivance need not endure. Finally, it will end because God has set in motion, soon or late, promises that will be kept. We grow cold and cynical. And we forget. But it is so. We are not conformers to this age, but we are the ones who gamble toward a new age of justice.

> *Soon or late, we know your promises will be kept,*
> *O God. We know that a new earth follows in the*
> *wake of your new heaven, and so we wait with*
> *eager longing. Keep us attentive to your rule.*
> *Empower us to overcome unjust contrivances and*
> *gamble toward your newness. Amen.*

Beyond All Our Expectations

The true light, which enlightens everyone, was
coming into the world.

He was in the world, and the world came
into being through him; yet the world did not
know him. He came to what was his own, and his
own people did not accept him. But to all who
received him, who believed in his name, he gave
power to become children of God, who were
born, not of blood or of the will of the flesh or of
the will of man, but of God.

And the Word became flesh and lived among
us, and we have seen his glory, the glory as of a
father's only son, full of grace and truth.

—John 1:9–14

There was something unroyal about him: no pretense,
no ambition, no limousine, no army, no coercion,
no royal marking. Wise and intelligent people are turned
toward the regal. Kings and prophets want to penetrate
the mystery. But the Jesus who showed up amid royal
hopes and royal songs was of another ilk, *powerful in
weakness, rich in poverty, wise in foolishness*, confounding
the wisdom of the Greeks and bewildering the Jews.

He is beyond all usual categories of power, because
he embodies the gentle, gracious, resilient, demanding
power of God. He does not trifle in temples and cities and
dynasties but in the power and truth of the creator God.

But John does not linger over Christology. He rushes on to the disciples. You disciples, you have seen. You have known; you have been in his presence. You have been healed and fed by him. You have tasted his bread and drunk his wine. *You know!*

- You know about life rooted in the spirit of God and not in the spirit of the age of violence.
- You know about the poor and have not had your head turned by wealth and power.
- You know about the impulse of creation toward health, a creaturely health signed in bread and wine. You know.

And because you know, you keep on singing. You can keep singing. You can keep hoping. And because you sing and hope, you can act in freedom, unburdened, unco-erced, unafraid, and without cynicism. The song goes on. It is a subversive, revolutionary song. And we, given access to this odd king, get to sign on to sing and to live it unafraid!

> *God of joy and hope, you come to us in Jesus*
> *as a king who overturns all our ordinary*
> *understandings of power. Your presence is*
> *unexpected and unsettling, but we know you, for*
> *we have known your healing and provision. Open*
> *our hearts to keep on singing and hoping, that we*
> *may live and act without fear. Amen.*

Week Four

A Love Letter concerning a Work in Progress

I thank my God every time I remember you,
constantly praying with joy in every one of my
prayers for all of you, because of your sharing
in the gospel from the first day until now. I am
confident of this, that the one who began a good
work among you will bring it to completion by
the day of Jesus Christ.
—Philippians 1:3–6

How would you like a love letter addressed to you in Advent, in anticipation of Christmas? That is what we have in the Epistle to the Philippians, Paul's love letter to his friends in the church in Philippi. It is a marvelous guideline in Advent for Christmas preparation:

It affirms that our lives are *bracketed by the big drama of God's purposes* and we do well to ponder such deep beginnings and such awesome culminations. Imagine God's large purposes hovering around your life.

Paul becomes specific in his wondrous phrasing about the *"in between"* that is our Advent work. Clearly, in between we have unfinished business, "we" being a work in process. But this is the way with love letters; we always know that the one addressed is not yet finished but still a work in process. And we intend to provide support along the way for a wondrous conclusion to the beloved.

Paul finishes by affirming that *all this will converge* in "glory and praise of God" (v. 11).

This Advent practice, in sum, is about ceding ourselves over to God in gladness, to refer our life back to God, who has given it to us.

What strikes me about this Advent love letter is this. When Paul writes the church, he assumes that Christmas preparation is serious business. But it has nothing to do with how the world lives with that commercial orgy. It is rather that when our lives are set in God's great drama, we have a quite different agenda. It is a profound agenda, because it touches the deep reality of how we are to live in God's mercy. It will be a prayer we pray for each other that we have enough resolve not to get caught up in the orgy but to create time and energy and space for a serious Advent. The urgent question always in the final days of Advent is: "Are you ready yet?"

Are you ready with overflowing love? Are you ready with knowledge and insight? Are you ready with purity and blamelessness? Are you ready with a harvest of righteousness?

No, not ready yet . . . but under way toward the great day of fullness. God will bring our life to completion. We may be glad and grateful as we wait.

> *Coming God, make us ready with overflowing love. May we be on the way to you even as you are on the way to us. May we be glad and grateful as we wait. Amen.*

A New Decision

> In that region, there were shepherds living in the fields, keeping watch over their flock by night. Then an angel of the Lord stood before them, and the glory of the Lord shone around them, and they were terrified. But the angel said to them, "Do not be afraid; for see—I am bringing you good news of great joy for all the people: to you is born this day in the city of David a Savior, who is the Messiah, the Lord."
>
> —Luke 2:8–11

Christmas is the celebration of the new decision of God. You know that decision well: "to you is born this day in the city of David a Savior, who is the Messiah, the Lord" (v. 11). Not Caesar in Rome, not Herod in Jerusalem, not Pilate as governor, not all the presidents and premiers and executives and generals, not any of them will be king, because the world has been turned a new way. It has been turned so that a king shall come from Bethlehem, not from the great city, but from a little city filled with filth and poverty.

But think what it means. It means, to anybody who knows, that the promises of God have been kept. He is faithful. He has not reneged. For a thousand years earlier he has said, I will keep this royal family and this royal promise and this royal vision. I will send the true David, and he will turn the world back to its sanity. Where there has been fear, he will bring joy. Where there has been oppression, he will bring justice. Where there has been suffering and sorrow, he will bring wholeness.

All the kings of the world hustled to keep their thrones. They are panic-stricken powers, scared of everything and everyone, but they don't know how to work at it except to kill and destroy, and our whole human history is like that.

Except God has made a fresh decision, and this new one does not come as threat but as child. He does not come as victory but as helpless child. He does not come in pride but in a way almost unnoticed by the world. But he is king. He is not robed in splendor but in baby clothes. He is not in the royal nursery but in a barn. None of it makes any sense. At least it does not make sense to people who think they have all of life reduced to a pattern and a formula.

The Christmas event in Bethlehem makes no sense unless you allow that it is a fresh decision from God himself about the new shape of the world. All of that came with the new announcement of the king. And then that messenger was joined by the chorus of angels who gave the theme of the divine decision: glory and peace.

Maybe you think angels are a little primitive, but it is one symbolic attempt to talk about God's new program coming to us. Christmas is a time for leaving our sober, sane world of budgets and schedules and rules and for just a moment blowing our minds with the thought that God intends other ways for us to live.

> *Break into our staid lives with the power of*
> *your holiness. Break up our old patterns and*
> *expectations, and transform us through the good*
> *news brought by the singing of angels: "to you is*
> *born this day in the city of David a Savior, who is*
> *the Messiah, the Lord." Amen.*

The Fidelity of God

Your steadfast love, O LORD, extends to the
heavens,
    your faithfulness to the clouds.
Your righteousness is like the mighty
mountains,
    your judgements are like the great deep;
    you save humans and animals alike, O LORD.
How precious is your steadfast love, O God!
    All people may take refuge in the shadow of
your wings.
                    —Psalm 36:5–7

Psalm 36 plunges us into the reality of faith. At its
very center, the psalm voices a glad affirmation that
is always again our beginning point in faith. The psalm
begins by remarking about God's own character and
God's own way in the world. Faith cannot begin with us,
either to celebrate us, or to commiserate about us, or to
claim for us.

Faith begins in this daring affirmation about God.
What a mouthful it is about God: Your steadfast love . . .
your utter reliability, your faithfulness . . . your solidarity, your righteousness . . . your will for our good. There
is nothing modest or embarrassed or subdued about this
claim. The psalmist believes that God's capacity for fidelity fills the whole of creation, the heavens, the clouds,
the mountains, so that all of life is redefined apart from

scientific, geological, measurable, controllable objects into the categories of relationship. The world is perceived as a very different sort of place, in which all issues, public and personal, religious and economic, all have to do with fidelity.

God's faithfulness is the chief desire, the central yearning, of our life. The speaker's exuberance invites us to reflect on the decisive yearning and driving desire of our lives, what we want, and what we will have when we have our life made whole. This voice believes that all our other yearnings are second level, not nearly so important as this central reality of God's good faithfulness.

This reliable God provides a safe place in which to hide, a welcome retreat from all the threats of life and of death. The poet, against all the threats of life, pictures God as the embracing, protecting, encompassing mother hen, the guarding eagle who extends wings and offers a safe place to hide.

What an alternative! Not to hide in our achievements, nor in our virtue, nor in our possessions, nor in our looks, nor in our technology, all of which are enormously precarious and short term, but to hide in God's cosmic practice of fidelity, to be safe there from every threat and anxiety and fear. The psalm engages us in an act of imagination out beyond the daily reality of threat to the possibility of safe communion.

> *Faithful God, your fidelity is the foundation*
> *of our hope in a new world that is coming, for*
> *your word is sure. Reorient our lives around this*
> *transformative truth: that we find our safety and*
> *our future in you alone. Amen.*

An Intrusive Absence

> Lo, I will send you the prophet Elijah before the great and terrible day of the LORD comes. He will turn the hearts of parents to their children and the hearts of children to their parents, so that I will not come and strike the land with a curse.
>
> —Malachi 4:5–6

These two verses are not at the end of the Jewish Bible, which is organized differently, but our Christian arrangement accepts that in this text we are at the brink of newness that cannot quite be seen. The text has God say it this way: "I will send you Elijah before the day of the Lord." So, in a way, we are in *the Elijah season.*

That means that you cannot understand what time it is, unless you know about Elijah, a key character in the Old Testament whom we mostly neglect. He appeared in an ancient time, not unlike our own, when the public scene was falling apart and the leadership failed. He did amazing things in that ancient time, ferocious, uncompromising, healing things that most people thought were impossible. He had uncommon powers, and he used them to the full.

He upset everything, healed things, made a difference. And they kept remembering him; they kept thinking about him; they kept wishing for him . . .

The more they thought about this Elijah who had marked their past so decisively, they were sure this same Elijah would mark their futures. They knew a big upheaval was coming, because things could not go on this way. And they had heard God say: I will send Elijah before the great day. He will be back to finish what he started. And then there is this amazing anticipation: He will turn the hearts of parents to their children and the hearts of children to their parents, so that I will not come and strike the land with a curse. He will reconcile the generations. He will heal our families of old and young, poor and rich, of have-nots and haves.

Everybody knows the world is at an edge. Everybody knows about the violence and abuse and exploitation. Everybody knows the world in our very moment is sick to death. But we are the ones who know he will come, called Elijah, called John, called Advent, called newness, a massive change. Because we believe that quite specifically, we celebrate Advent, which is the sense of being at the edge of newness. We are the only ones who believe that. Ancient Greeks did not believe it. And contemporary cynics do not believe it. That is what makes so many of us so resigned, so filled with despair, so selfish, so greedy, so anxious . . . because the world is hopeless.

But we are not hopeless. We are at the break of God's future. The Lord will come in power and in grace, to turn the hearts of the children and to turn the hearts of the parents, to turn us from despair and anger and brutality and greed and fear. We celebrate because we expect and await the turn.

> *God of newness, turn us from despair, anger,*
> *brutality, greed, and fear. Bring healing to our*
> *families and communities. Bring healing to our*
> *own hearts that we may hold fast to the hope that*
> *the world is about to turn. Amen.*

What Time Is It?

Therefore the Lord himself will give you a sign.
Look, the young woman is with child and shall
bear a son, and shall name him Immanuel.
—Isaiah 7:14

When Joseph awoke from sleep, he did as the
angel of the Lord commanded him; he took her
as his wife, but had no marital relations with her
until she had borne a son; and he named him
Jesus.
—Matthew 1:24–25

These two texts are about two odd babies, Immanuel
and Jesus. The two texts are about two mothers, a
young woman whose name we do not know and a virgin
who has not married. The two texts are about threats to
two world empires, Assyria and Rome. The texts show
how power shifts from the empire to the baby. The
empires, in fear and enmity, do not know what time it is.
But the clock carried by the baby keeps ticking away.

What time is it? Time for peace, time for justice, time
for land reform, time for health care, time for Jubilee
year, time for miraculous feeding, time for comfort, time
for freedom. *Tick tock, tick tock.* The empire cannot find
the clock, cannot stop the baby, cannot have its way, cannot keep its own regime in place.

Imagine the superpowers of the world. Imagine the

great corporate executives and all the people of harsh power in industry and schools and churches and banks and armies and tax offices who are used to having their way. Imagine the repressive part of our own lives, which are used to the silencing and crushing. Imagine all those threatened powers listening to the clock of the babies, moving relentlessly to the ending and transformation and beginnings.

This is the miracle of the babies. Because the baby has come by the spirit, the world is changed. The empires are on notice. The kingdoms are under threat. A little baby offers another way in the world that destabilizes and invites us to new trust and new freedom. So be asking in Advent, "What time is it?" Well, it depends. If you think the empire is in charge, it is anytime. If you bet on the baby, it is very late, very close, very dangerous.

Bet on the baby. Get free of the coercive power of the empire. Then act differently about power and money and land and justice and homes and food and health care. Bet on the baby and notice the new world in which we live where the empires have been subverted. Bet on the baby and listen to the clock ticking away.

> *O God, our lives are shaped by the times of empire, so much so that we can barely hear the "tick tock tick tock" of your time. During this Advent season may we once again bet on the baby. May we know the time and so live with hope and justice. Amen.*

Living and Thinking
in Transformative Ways

Do not be overcome by evil, but overcome evil
with good.

Romans 12:21

W hat counts for a Christian is how one lives. We are
called by the gospel to live a different kind of life,
to be engaged in the world and in the neighborhood in
transformative ways.

That is why Paul, after he makes his complex theological argument, ends in Romans 12 with a quite specific
inventory of how Christians are to live in the world and
in the neighborhood.

Paul says: *Live in generosity as a giver*. Paul knows that
those who live in the gospel have been given an abundance of life, and they are to let that abundance from God
spill over into the life of the neighborhood. That abundance among us is very often a material blessing, and it
is to be shared. But it is also a generosity of spirit that
reaches out, by its very openness, to let one's presence
and attitude be a blessing to others around.

Paul writes: *Extend hospitality to strangers*. The stranger
is somewhat different for us now, as we are variously
preoccupied with differences in ethnicity, in gender, in
nationality, in religious passion, or even in class. It is easy
enough to be suspicious of strangers and to stay with
one's own kind and exclude the others if we can. But Paul
knows that in fact we are all strangers and aliens in the

world, and we have been wrapped in God's goodness that gives us freedom to practice hospitality to others, so that they may be welcome and make a home in our midst and be with us in the neighborhood of God.

Paul writes: *Never avenge yourselves.* He knows about trying to get even. He urges his fellow Christians instead to break that vicious cycle of getting even, to transform the thirst for vengeance into acts of forgiveness, so that one no longer needs to get even. Such a transformative act impacts both parties in healing ways, the one forgiven and the one who forgives.

There is more that Paul highlights, but what a place to start: generosity, hospitality, forgiveness.

When we resolve to live that way, the neighborhood is transformed.

> *You call us to overcome evil with good, to live a different kind of life than the one offered to us by the world. During this time of waiting, stir anew our commitment to generosity and hospitality and forgiveness, that we might be people of hope and healing in the neighborhoods of our lives. Amen.*

Celebrating the Revolution

Who is like the LORD our God,
   who is seated on high,
who looks far down
   on the heavens and the earth?
He raises the poor from the dust,
   and lifts the needy from the ash heap,
to make them sit with princes,
   with the princes of his people.
He gives the barren woman a home,
   making her the joyous mother of children.
Praise the LORD!

                    —Psalm 113:5–9

O f all the words of Scripture that make God visible in the world, none is more dangerous or welcome—depending on who we are—than Psalm 113. At the center of the psalm are some of the most stunning words we have about God, lined out in lyrical fashion: God *raises* the poor from the dust; God *lifts* the needy from the ash heap; God *makes* them sit with princes; God *gives* the barren woman a home.

Through this series of active verbs, God is said to be at work turning the world upside down, revamping the economy, reordering the values of domestic life. The words exhibit God as the prime mover in a revolutionary transformation of the way money and power work in the world.

The psalm undoubtedly reflects the joy and astonishment of people in that ancient world who were helpless and powerless and in despair. And then, in ways they do not explain, they found the world revised. And they credited that revision to God. This psalm is the celebration voiced by the *poor* who are invited back into the economy. It is the voice of the *needy* on the ash heap who sound like ancient street people. It is the song of *barren women* who were shamed in the ancient world for not producing children. They all find a new lease on life, because the God of the Gospel would not let any of God's precious children—the needy, the poor, the barren—be second-class citizens who had to live in shame and poverty. People like us may find such a song a jolt, because we have settled for a more timid God; but this is the one shown us in the text!

The psalm speaks against our settled worlds. It would take practice to learn to sing this way, to sing about the revolution that God is undertaking that centers in Jesus; but unless we sing and live that song, we settle, against the gospel, for the world the way it is. The news of Advent is that God is on the loose and appearing soon in unexpected places.

> *Unsettling God, help us to sign on to your*
> *dangerous and welcome good news. May our*
> *celebrations be marked by protest and by praise—*
> *protest against all that diminishes life and stands*
> *in the way of your coming in mercy, praise that*
> *you are on the loose and appearing soon. Amen.*

A New World Birthed

> But just when he had resolved to do this, an angel
> of the Lord appeared to him in a dream and said,
> "Joseph, son of David, do not be afraid to take
> Mary as your wife, for the child conceived in her
> is from the Holy Spirit."
>
> —Matthew 1:20

What a mouthful! It is, moreover, a mouthful from an angel, a messenger of God, one sent from heaven to earth, a message from the outside not given in human terms, not given in earthly terms, not given according to Joseph's normal assumptions. The angel spoke in a dream, not when Joseph could be awake and in control.

So notice first that the expectation of Jesus is outside all our categories, given by God's rule in God's own way. Our way in response to this text is not to explain; it is, rather, to be dazzled that at Christmas something happens beyond all our calculations. This is a baby and a wonder and a gift that are designed to move us beyond ourselves.

Notice second that the baby has no father. But notice that is not the point. Rather the emphasis is that the baby is from the Holy Spirit. We may set aside a lot of silly arguments and speculation about biological transactions and notice, rather, that newness comes when God's spirit stirs beyond everything that has been settled:

- It is God's spirit that hovered in Genesis 1 to greet a new world, a new heaven, and a new earth where there had been none.
- It is God's spirit, God's wind that blows the waters back in Egypt and lets our ancestors go free.
- It is God's spirit that called apostles and prophets and martyrs beyond themselves to do dangerous acts of obedience.
- It was God's spirit that came upon the disciples in the book of Acts and created a new community of faith and power and obedience and mission.
- It is God's spirit that begins something new when the world is exhausted, when our imagination fails and our lives shut down in silence and despair.

That is what happened here; God's spirit stirred and caused something deeply new in the world. The healing, transforming, creating wind of God has caused a new baby who will change everything among us.

The gift of Christmas contradicts everything we sense about our own life. Our world feels unsavable, and here is the baby named Jesus, "Save." Our world and our lives often feel abandoned, and here is the baby named Immanuel, "God with us." Be ready to have your sense of the world contradicted by this gift from God. Rest on the new promise from the angel that you may be safe and whole and generous.

Coming Son of God, blowing spirit of God,
hovering Father God, once again you come to
us in newness, stirring up beauty and life and
love beyond our calculations or control. May
we be dazzled by the mystery of your abundant
generosity. May we rest in the promise, and may
we share the promise with a weary world. Amen.

I Am about to Do a New Thing

> Do not remember the former things,
>   or consider the things of old.
> I am about to do a new thing;
>   now it springs forth, do you not perceive it?
> I will make a way in the wilderness
>   and rivers in the desert.
>   —Isaiah 43:18–19

C hristmas is especially for those of us whose lives are
scarred and hurt in debilitating ways. Of course that
means all of us. You see, Christmas is not finally about a
baby and all of that romantic business. Christmas is about
a word from God addressed to the world in its exhaus-
tion. This word from the book of Isaiah is addressed to
displaced persons who were mired down, and beaten, and
about to give up. They kept playing old songs and going
over and over and over the old hurts and old quarrels and
old failures and old sins and old defeats.

The word of God at Christmas, for all those who are
disqualified, is in two simple parts.

The first part is this: *Do not remember former things.*
Think how much energy we use on "former things." We
may do this in two ways, neither of which helps us. We
may remember "good old days," back when it was all
right, and we remember with such yearning and nostalgia
and romance. We likely remember things as much better than they really were. Or conversely, we remember

all the negatives. We go over the past in shame, wishing we had not said what we said or had not done what we did. We know our guilt, and we go over it, or we remember how hurt we were, and angry, and we remember how badly we were treated. We enjoy the past either way, in anger or in guilt, because it is so precious to us, and we treasure our hurt.

But then the gospel comes! *Do not remember former things*. Christmas, when God speaks clearly and when God acts decisively, is a time for letting go and forgetting and giving up and releasing all that is past.

The second part of this word from God, spoken on Christmas day, is this: *Behold I am doing a new thing*. That word is the central fact of the Bible and the key to our gospel faith. That is the good news for us. The reason we may forget what is old and past is that it is being powerfully displaced by what is new and healing and liberating. The poet adds, with a little impatience, "Do you not perceive it?" Haven't you noticed the newness God is working? Christmas is a day to stop and notice the newness that God is giving, that lets our life start over in a fresh place.

The newness that God wrought at Christmas was sending into the world this Jesus who is beyond our imagination, who brought healing and grace everywhere he went, who forgave and transformed and called people out beyond themselves to a newness they could not have imagined. "I am doing a new thing!"

> *It is easy for us to be held down and held back by the pain or glories of the past. Aid us in perceiving the wondrous new thing you are doing in our world through the birth of Jesus, the one who comes to make all things new. Amen.*

Prayers for the Christmas Season

No Room!

On this holy Christmas Day
  we remember the innkeeper in Bethlehem,
  the one who turned the couple away.
He said, "Sorry, full up; no room!"
We do not know: perhaps he was full, but perhaps he
  turned away such disheveled, weary, poverty-stricken
  customers as bad for business.
If so, "no room" was only an excuse.
We know about such excuses:
  No room for immigrants;
  No room for gays.
  Before that, no room for blacks.
  Before that, no room for women.
But Christ squeezed in anyway, made room in the inn, in
the village of Bethlehem, and in the world. The Christ
Child defied the verdict of "no room" and made room for
many more.
  We promise, dear Christ child, that we will make room
  as did you,
    Even for those who are so unlike us. Amen.

An Executive Order

On this second day of Christmas, we remember that Caesar (the emperor) decreed everyone to go back to home base. He would count people for tax purposes and to mobilize the army draft.

The holy couple obeyed. But their obedience became awesome subversion, for they brought with them the Christ child, who defied such imperial decrees for the sake of the governance that he would initiate.

We also live amid executive orders from empires of war and money. But we know better!

We resolve, dear Christ Child,

to notice our ambiguity about such edicts,

to watch for places of alternative obedience, and

finally, to refuse Caesar's authority over us.

We give you thanks for your always-coming kingdom. Amen.

Third Day of Christmas

We Must Do Something

On this third day of Christmas we remember the inn-keeper declaring, "No room." His wife heard him and grimaced. She knew better. She knew that after "business":

There is hospitality.

There is welcome to the stranger.

There is respect for those unlike us.

She blurted out, "We must do something!" He grudgingly opened his barn and provided straw.

We resonate with the wife of the innkeeper, because we also know there is more than "business." We remember your word, dear Christ Child:

"I was a stranger and you welcomed me.

As you did it to the least . . ."

We are invited to know better like the wife; to act, even if grudgingly, like her husband. We resolve on this holy day that we must do something to welcome the stranger in our midst. Amen.

Joining the Conversation

On this fourth day of Christmas, we watch the Bethlehem
   scene:
   The innkeeper sullen as he provides straw.
   The wife of the innkeeper providing what comfort she
could, providing "swaddling clothes" and treating the
shabby couple as guests.
We observe the tense interaction between
   the sullen straw-provider and
   the one who gives aid to the desperate couple.
It is a conversation, always going on among us between
   what is smart and
   what is wise.
We live out that conversation all the time:
   Smart or wise?
   Wise or smart?
And we remember the scandalous good news:
   "The foolishness of God is wiser than human wisdom."
We pray for courage and resolve to be foolish while the
world presses us to be smart. Amen.

What Child Is This?

Father Joseph was a good man. He would do the right
thing for Mary, instructed by an angel.
He arrived at the inn, gathered straw, and watched while
the baby was born. He must have wondered,
    What child is this?
        The baby of a virgin,
        the outcome of conception from the Holy Spirit,
        a baby full of "grace and truth"?
        Later on, "God from God, Light from Light, true
            God from true God . . ."
It was a scandal that would, in the wisdom of the church,
be made into a mystery.
We are like Joseph, dear Christ Child, on this fifth day of
Christmas,
    discomfited by the scandal of your life,
    but willing to trust that scandal as a mystery,
        a mystery that defies our certitude,
        a wonder that transforms the world,
        a miracle that makes all things new,
        a gift beyond our explanation.
We give thanks for Joseph and all who trust and obey.
Amen.

Holy News in a So-So Village

On this sixth day of Christmas we remember that the
angels showed up for work on the first Noel.
God dispatched them specifically to Bethlehem, an
out-of-the way village south of Jerusalem to proclaim
God's glory. They wondered about that. Better to
bring the message to Jerusalem, or Damascus, or
Tyre, or Nineveh.
But they obeyed.
Then the Holy One added to the message: "Declare
peace on earth for all humanity."
They obeyed, went to Bethlehem, and filled the sky
with song:
"Glory to God in the highest and peace on earth, good
will to humanity."
Along with the shepherds, we hear their song.
It is partly a declaration: there will be and is glory in
heaven and peace on earth.
But it is also a summons: a call to praise God and do
peace.
Do praise with your tongue, do peace with your feet.
We give you thanks for such good angelic words among
us. Amen.

Hunkered Down in the Citadel

On this seventh day of Christmas we remember how the news of "Emmanuel" reached Jerusalem, citadel of power, wealth, and control. King Herod was hunkered down there in fear, caught between Roman supervision and potential Jewish uprising. He received news of the birth with lethal anxiety.

We confess to you, dear Christ Child, that we are much in the same boat. We also, as we are able, gather in our citadels of power, wealth, and control. We count on

a strong economy,

a dominant military, and

a patriotic orthodoxy.

We are fearful and resist any glint of newness.

Even so, we cannot take our eyes off the scene in Bethlehem. We know, down below our anxiety, that something decisive has changed. We know that this baby brings promises that Herod cannot void. The baby brings demands that we cannot evade. Even in our paralyzing anxiety, we keep an eye on the baby who comes as threat and possibility. Amen.

In the Winter of Our Discontent

Despite global warming, we still sing, "In the Bleak Midwinter." We do so because "bleakness" is not from snow and cold. It is winter among us: the chill of anxiety, the freeze of fear, the iciness of hate, the frigidness of exclusion and violence. Our discontent causes us to retreat into our comfort zones of tribe and mantra that exclude all "others."

In the bleakness of midwinter came God incarnate,
>   warming away winter anxiety,
>   thawing us away from winter fear,
>   melting us away from winter hate, and
>   breaking the frozen winter violence among us,

so that our winter of discontent may end.
We give thanks on this eighth day of Christmas that the Christ child came powerfully into the bleakness.
The carol says that the Christ child will have "my heart,"
>   even more my life,
>   thus an end to our winter of discontent. Amen.

Ninth Day of Christmas

A Village Nine Miles Away

In Upware, England, there is a pub called "Five Miles from Anywhere." Bethlehem is like that, nine miles from Jerusalem, nine miles from importance or power, "little among the clans of Judah." Now it is filled with fearful Palestinians on watch because of ominous Israeli surveillance. This "little town of Bethlehem" is replicated in many out-of-the-way places where nobody important ever goes, where there are no possibilities or hopes but only subsistence, vigilance, and fear. We know about such places that are remote from significance, forgotten and vulnerable.

On this ninth day of Christmas, we give you thanks that in such a place "the wondrous gift is given." The gift is

the wonder of the Christ child,
the miracle of new possibility,
the spectacle of opening a new future,

all given in the silence. Bethlehem does not remain unvisited. The vulnerable are not forgotten; the future is not closed. Little Bethlehem is the matrix of God's newness. Amen.

Tongue and Feet!

Martin Luther King insisted we must "pray with our feet." This is the exact claim of the carol "Go, Tell It on the Mountain" (an allusion to Isaiah 40:9, "Get you up to a high mountain"). On this tenth day of Christmas we receive two imperatives. First, tell! Speak it with our tongues; voice the gospel of the Christ child. The rulers of this age want us silenced, subdued, and submissive. But tell an alternative story of justice and peace. Second, go! That is the "feet" part. "Go" means to leave our comfort zone, to invest our bodies, to act truth to power wherever power serves injustice.

We have tongues to tell and feet to go! We may, from this day, go and tell,

that Jesus Christ is born,

that God sent salvation that blessed Christmas morn,

that the new world is open for business.

The new truth is peace and justice from the lowly manger to lowly folk, echoing the angel chorus. Amen.

Adore in Abandonment

On this eleventh day of Christmas, "all ye faithful" are invited to come. The "all" who are invited include the poor, the crippled, the lame, the blind, the forgotten, the marginalized, the vulnerable, the fearful, the anxious, the weary . . . well, all of us! The single requirement is that we be faithful, that we bet on this baby, that we trust this wonder that escapes our explanation.

We are invited to come to Bethlehem, where Herod and Caesar will never go, the shabby place where comes God from God,
Light from Light,
True God from true God,
begotten not made.
When we come, we are only to "adore." "Adore" is beyond love, trust, or obey. It is an emotional rush of abandonment that gives over everything in gratitude and awe. "Adore" is to abandon common sense and be silly in treasuring, as in first love. That is what we do on this eleventh day.

We come to this shabby place. We are faithful, and we adore. By sundown we may say, "I don't know what came over me!" Amen.

Pondering

To "ponder" is to hold an idea that keeps on, over and over and over. Mother Mary did that. She pondered "all these words."

She pondered Gabriel's announcement.

She pondered Joseph's generosity.

She pondered the song of the angels and the visit of the shepherds.

She sensed these events were freighted with long-term truthfulness.

On this twelfth day of Christmas, we may, with Mother Mary "ponder all these things," engage in slow rumination because we cannot dispose of them, or explain them, or decode them.

We will hold them in consciousness even in a world where interest spans last only thirteen seconds and we delete and move on. We will linger there, confident that the sum of these events yields a new world. We will keep them in our hearts as she did, the place where we

make new resolves,

run fresh risks, and

embrace new lives.

From this twelfth day, we linger there for many more days to come. Amen.